I0086714

Owl Howse Press

(W)hole

From Absence
To Abundance

Poems
Of Recovery and Faith
From

Stevie G

(W)HOLE: FROM ABSENCE TO ABUNDANCE, POEMS OF RECOV-
ERY AND FAITH. Copyright © 2013 with original Library of Congress
Copyright © 2010 by Stevie G. All rights reserved. Printed in the United
States of America. No part of this book may be used or reproduced in any
manner whatsoever without written permission except in the case of brief
quotations embodied in critical articles and reviews. For information contact
Owl Howse Press at info@poetstevieg.com.

LIMITED FIRST EDITION

Published 2013

Library of Congress cataloging-in-Publication Data

G, Stevie
Whole: From Absence to Abundance : poems/Stevie G

ISBN-13 978-0615935935 (Owl Howse Press)
ISBN-10 0615935931
United States Copyright Office Registration Number: TXu 1-634-930

I want to know if you can sit with pain, mine or your own, without moving to hide it or fade it or fix it ...

I want to know if you can be with joy, mine or your own; if you can dance with wildness and let the ecstasy fill you ...

It doesn't interest me who you are, or how you came to be here – I want to know if you will stand in the center of the fire with me and not shrink back.

- Oriah Mountain Dreamer, *The Invitation*

For Vicky,
Niko and Alexcito

Your
hot feet
melt me

PREFACE

Thank You God
For Being Here
With Me Now

Not so long ago, upon reading words like these, I would have quickly closed this book, put it back on the shelf, and walked away, shaking my head in pity ... suppressing with a dismissive snort that nagging doubt about my inner skeptic's constant doubting, extinguishing with a sneer that spark of longing for something more, throwing another shovelful of disdain on that silent seed of belief suffocating in the sarcophagus of my soul.

I had no need of a power greater than myself. God, and especially religion, I saw as signs of human weakness, of ignorance, of rigidity and hypocritical righteousness.

A de facto atheist, or agnostic at best, I was raised without even passing reference to spirituality and carefully taught from an early age that I had to "figure it out for myself." Trusting others or trusting *in* "something other than" was more than just strange, it was dangerous.

Not aware of a reality other than the one I was in, I was a guppy swimming in waters which surrounded me with this simple message: "How give of yourself with abandon when abandonment is inevitable?" So then, and throughout my life, I would always hold something back, guarding jealously my reserves, as I couldn't count on anyone or anything else to be there for me ... but me.

It's ironic that of all life's battles, the most brutal and destructive one is the one we don't even know we're in. Though ugly and horrendously painful, the acute misfortunes others have faced in their lives – such as parental desertion or crushing poverty, physical, mental or sexual abuse – have at the very least given them a visible enemy to point the finger at and engage.

In contrast, detachment and emotional deprivation are especially slippery foes to fight. Taking on the "lack of" something is like trying to prove the negative. Though all may have been sunshine and smiles on the surface – parents in attendance, stable household, trappings of modest middle-class comfort and accomplishment – many of us forever walked in a fog, paralyzed with fear and resentment.

The warriors of absence would creep stealthily into our young bones like termites – this lack of attachment in our primary relationships eating away at our timbers from the inside out. We may have continued appearing stable and put together on the outside, sometimes through old age and even death. But within, our beams weakened, we crumbled to dust and were lost.

Without a solid center – that deep place where early on one is mirrored and appreciated, allowed to fail in safety and succeed in joy, and either way be held dearly in love – we had neither practice of- nor tools for reaching out. In our fear of rejection, we would rarely if ever make meaningful connections, then or later. Not with others, nor with God, nor with ourselves.

Often before learning to talk, the covert emotional neglect we experienced (just like that overt abuse others encountered) hollowed out our core – that secure sense of our self and our place in the world. And, as nature abhors a vacuum, numbness, despair and often addiction rushed in to fill the void.

With feelings of unworthiness and shame further isolating us, we would soon forget our past, turn from our future, and, most tragically, miss each moment of our present. Always elsewhere – yearning for something we never got, something which we'd often be unaware we were even yearning for – we were never in the here, never in the now.

Sometimes loving family, trusted friends, or caring acquaintances might intervene before we caused irreparable damage to ourselves and others. But often they would not, could not – especially for those of us skilled in the deception of projecting perfection. And so we would lose, or almost lose, everything near and dear to us.

We would fall. Sometimes hard.

And looking back, count it a blessing.

For if we had the good fortune to be appropriately humbled by this experience, we finally would be given the opportunity to slowly and painfully discover – with serendipity and God's grace – that we could not, and can not, do it alone. We could not, and can not figure it out for ourselves. And we never were, nor are now, in charge.

Trying to find solid ground on which to rebuild our collapsing lives, we would finally, *finally!*, learn to ask for help. And from that simple act, that sweet surrender, the foundation of our recovery and our faith would be laid.

Today, it may take many years and many stones to rebuild our damaged hearts, but in connecting – and in being *grateful* for these connections with others, with our world, with ourselves in the precious present, and, finally, with our God – we access that part of ourselves we always secretly longed for, but never dared believe in. Thankful to be moving from absence to abundance.

CONTENTS

Absence

Mom 1
Orbit.................................... 6
Empty 8
Unsaid.................................. 9
How 11
Wind 12
Bones 13
Boy....................................... 16
Just...................................... 18
Fear 22
Roots.................................... 27
Tantrum................................. 29
Surrogate................................ 32
Enemies 34
Sheep 36
Skin...................................... 40
Pair O' Docs 42

Abundance

Paradox 53
Align 62
Waltz 65
Fearless 70
Moment 71
Tortuga 72
Cama 74
Dawn 75
Vicky 76
Niko 77
Alexcito 78
Sole 79
Breathe 83
Faith 85
Dog 88
Cama^2 89
Sunday 90
Gorilla 92
Prescription 96
Belonging 97
Abandon 99
Tetherball 102
How Much I Love You 104

Absence

Mom

(In 2003 my mother suffered a major stroke that left her bedridden, paralyzed on her right side and semi-vegetative, though ironically able to sing the songs of her youth and to cry with abandon. While this poem was written during the second year of her being in this state, she lay that way 7 more, locked in her failing mind and frozen muscles, until peacefully letting go in February, 2012.)

PROLOGUE

I'm writing in rhyme
'Cause it seems like time
In your last refrain
To explore the pain

After 85 years
You've melted
Awash in tears
You've felt it…

The hand of God…
Now stroking your cheek
Surrender now
Find the strength to be weak

MOM

Mom, are you lingering for me?
Because your soul seems set to go
Shed the body and be free
And in His presence finally "know"

At forty one I finally find
My feelings buried deep inside
Imprisoned long there by my mind
But now you've left I can't confide

That it's you who've taught me this
To rely upon my brain
Shut down what's in my heart
As it will only cause me pain

Yet I remember you *could* cry
Never Dad, I don't know why
And it seems that in *that* space
We could have found a higher place

Because my heart reached out to you
Longed to take away your pain
But the moment quickly flew
Lost, because you thought that it would "strain"

But so what if I was "burdened"
By your "inconvenient" feelings
At least then I would have felt
The real Mom with whom I'm dealing

NOW! In your absence
I am mad. *Goddammit*!
At you not being there
And I'm sad. *God bless it*!

That while you'd listen
You'd never really hear
And if you did
My lurking, scratching, frozen fear

Was that you wouldn't care
About the me that you'd find there
And so I'd talk and fill the gaps
The empty places on the map

So that I wouldn't feel uncomfortable
Ignore the yawning void
Like a fog, I couldn't see
And that feeling I'd avoid

For if you never really saw *me*
It begs the question, "Why?"
Was I not good enough for you
Did you *never* see me fly?

Oh why, oh why, oh why, oh why
Did you not yell it to the heavens?!?
"He's mine!" Shout it loud!
"I'm on cloud nine. He makes me proud!"

For with *my* boys I daily marvel
At the miracle they are
And pray that in their precious presence
That I will finally find *my* star

My star! That was not in your eyes
Where it should have been
Instead the disappointed sighs
Stone walls that never let me in

And now… you've left again
But not this time with a book,
Macneil/Lehrer or Alistair Cooke

This time your disconnect is final
And the light I hoped to see as mine

Will never be there
And it's hard to say goodbye
When we never really said hello

To watch you cry
To let you go

Without giving you the comfort
That *I* so wanted

I stroke your forehead
You slap my hand away
I'm tempted just to say "Okay, good day!"
And then I stop and say "No way!"

I pray
I may
Be strong, to fight
And stay

Not go away

Like you did

The light in your eyes
Flickering out
And me as a boy
Wanting to shout

To reach in and grab it
And train it on me
"See me! Hear me!
You're apple I'll be!"

But that didn't happen
And the lesson I guess
Is to hold *myself* first
And then hold the rest

And also to let go in God's tender arms
Our Father in heaven (like Dad)
Where no harm

Can come unto me
If only I see
My soul on its journey
Will finally be free

To feel the embrace
The warmth on my face
The belonging in place
The warm blanket of grace

EPILOGUE
And someday you will find me
And I will find you
In morning fields of grass
Where the droplets of dew

Quietly gather together
Father Sun kissing their cheek
Rolling down to the Earth
Mother's bosom they seek

To be nourished
And grow
Become God
Feel the flow

And to finally know
That you love me
And I too
Love you so

Orbit

He circled her sun, then
Not mine
The force to which he bowed, was hers
Thus never did I shine

For him
Who needed desperately
To be
With someone
Finally
From his loneliness
To set him free

But stuffing self into *her* star
Took from me *my* center
And where he could have filled my core
Instead let coldness enter

For I was doubly second then
Satellite to his fawning moon
And I resent unfathered men
Like me for whom life plays no tune

For his song, had I heard it
From deep inside his embered heart
Would have just assured it -
My place on earth - secure, and not apart

So now I try to build
Upon his wobbly steps
Toward wholeness
Hope and right

And to my sons, I pray, bequeath
An orbit, near
That holds them dear
Until they feel God's tender might

Empty

Silent voices screaming out
Tomblike stillness shrouds his shouts
That child within who cries and pouts
But is not heard and hence must doubt

That what he needs will ever be
Of interest, or that his pleas
Will find soft breast, or that he'll see,
Like all the rest, himself … set free.

And so the part of him that wants
Is buried deep, and deeply haunts
Him in his sleep, and tests and taunts
Him, and he weeps for love so daunt-

Ing, guarded, locked, in gray stone cell –
Affection craved. And thus he yells
Down dark, deprived and endless well.
His living grave. His private hell.

These shrill sharp whispers in his head
That bang against his walls of dread
Have left him numb, of all life bled
Shrieking fears best left unsaid

Unsaid

It was those words that were not said
That cleaved his heart from fretful head
And so he lay there, still, and bled
His spirit stayed, his soul unfed

It was blackmail, not bribery
Looking back now I find
"Harsh" you say? This assessment of my source?
Well, apologies, but welcome to my mind

Seeing more clearly
How she withheld to get her way
This "absence of" emerging
From starved night to painful day

Not SMothered by a long shot
"Enmeshed?" I wish I got!
No, the search still lingers
For her kind, caressing fingers

Heart held hostage
Paying dearly for approval
Then mistaking it for love

Sunshine without smiles
So chained and frozen. Stuck.
Choked with slippery, silent gloves

The message then
Was loud and clear
"I'll love you most
When you're not here"

What should I have done? Why was *I* not enough?
What didn't I do? What chore did I cut?
Why can't I just be? Why is this now so rough?
Why can't I be free? Open heart, mind shut?

Stitching head and heart back together,
Now, as easy as catching a hurricane's feather
Essential I break the past's terrible tether
Let in blue skies. Let go stormy weather

Saying it now in the present, before I'm dead
Saying it now, so I don't feel the dread
Of not saying it now, of losing the thread,
Of waking in heaven
            My soul's poetry
                Unshed

How

The crushing isolation
From womb to world to tomb
The impenetrable silence
In his sad and lonely room

How overcome the vast indifference
Of his mother's stonewalled face
And assume his rightful place
Amongst the living human race?

He smelled sweet flowers once, the boy,
In his dad's caressing picture
How now convince the man
That this pure joy is still a fixture

In his life – his heart his soul,
His dreams, his hopes his goals?
And how to let the past be passed
And let the present fill this hole

Inside – the aching, yearning center –
Where no one he dare let enter
How let go of being apart and odd
Unworthy of a loving God

How? Someone tell me please!
I beseech on bent and bloodied knees
So tired and bruised from trying to please
Just how, just how can I unfreeze?

Wind

The boy sits in the campsite chair
Alone and listening for the air
To clue him, please, "Is Someone there?
More than just my brain's aware?"

Wishing for the wind
To stroke his face
      Envelop him in love
      That he so lacks
            But finds, sometimes
            In Nature's grace

Banished since birth by self-reliance,
There was no God to soothe him
Faith in something "higher than"
Lost to 70's praise of human groovin'

So his succor, then, when lost, afraid
Is found once yearly in State Park's glade
Shy connection, unconsciously made
With the whispers heard in Redwood's shade

Trying to earnestly decipher
Words slipping through soft stirring boughs
Almost grasping ... almost
The message that he belongs somehow

Bones

The skeletons come dance for me
With stunning regularity
Clattering from their cloistered closet
So I can clearly, plainly see
How their boisterous, bouncing bones
Have crumbled inside to dull debris

For did I have more sense of self
There'd be far fewer secrets
Hidden on my wardrobe's far back shelf
But without strong structure in my life
I've crossed boundaries better left uncrossed
And paid a pretty penny in spiritual strife

"I know it in my bones,"
Some people say with great conviction
But for those of us raised boneless
This cocky confidence
– "faith in oneself" –
Long ago fell to addiction

Addiction to the creature comforts
While our termite-gnawed timbers
We'd so nicely neglect
No brawny beam to balance pain-soaked roof
While scabrous skin self-flagellation
We'd prefer to perfect

Like amoeba recruits without strict orders
Our permeable flesh it has no borders
Flopping about
Like water balloons
We pray for a spine
But soon find we're buffoons

Dancing around
Like contortionist clowns
Seeking commitment
And certainty
Firm foundation
And guarantee

But getting instead
The bone-crushing dread
That far from
Securing our solid center
We are but lowly
Month-to-month renters

Our hopes of settling into a comfy core
Are bum-rushed rudely out the door

The shaky scaffold that I thus try to erect
Around my black hole, each and every day
Is built fast and loose,
A poor excuse
For strong and home-grown
Vertebrae

For just like we're given our inner flame
(Soon after we're given our very own name)
So our sturdy internal frame
Is nurtured and constructed
With precision just the same!
Truly, this is no child's game

Piece by tender, caring piece
Feet to ankles, calves to knees
Our portentous parents
(Whom we can't elect)
Need fortify this edifice
So we can stand erect

For without strong bones
We're pale copies, faded clones
No self concept
No clear zones
Boundary-less
And on our own

Not knowing where we end or start
Licking our wounded, fragile hearts
Not connecting,
Then, our goal
Our scoliosis
Of the soul

But Christ Almighty spare me this fate!
I'll grow my girders before it's too late
Substituting the fabrication
Of psycho/spiritual simulation
Filling in where forbears fell
Before I must ask for whom tolls the bell

So next time I see my skeleton dance
I'll invite him in, taking the chance
That he'll connect with my muddled middle
And hopefully, Oh hi diddle diddle,
Solve that really ridiculous riddle

  (Of how we survive
  Leading hollow lives
  Until we learn to patch our own porous fence
  Raise high the poles in our own deflated tents)

Rebuilding these beautiful
                  battered
                      bones
      … little
              by little
                  by little

15

Boy

Welling up at times
Despite the broken spine
That severed part
That cleaved head from youthful heart

The boy cries out to us
But like a rainy memory on a fading yellow bus
His shouts go unheard
The silent screams of a caged and dying bird

And the outrage bubbles and boils and builds
At the helpless child whom indifference killed
His blood, our blood, still being spilled
His grief, our grief, stuffed away by our will

Like my boy, told by Mom
"Figure it out for yourself"
World crumbling from under me
Stuck there, midair, till now, without help

Like yours, told by his
"Why you can't even play right!"
Spirit thoughtlessly crushed
Your day thrown into darkest night

Like yours with the shits
Til Dad came, smelling of beer
Your stomach in twisting, turning fits
Still spinning your plates from there to here

Or like your second grader
Who at some silly slight
Took on tormenting classmates
Then somehow lost your belly's fight

And like you, with your father's fists
Or you, with mother there, but missed
How did it all come down to this?
What healing is there in this ugly grist?

Oh yes, the rage is there
(Our hate turned in)
And it's just not fair
We *cannot* let it win

So we fight, me for you, you for me
We fight for our sons and family
We fight to mend our wounded souls
To coax them from hiding, these scared and lonely foals.

Like treehouse friends we sit and circle up
Pour out the pain that cracks our fragile cup
Connecting as we couldn't then
A brotherhood of broken men

And as the setting sun streaks 'cross the room
We feel the sadness, yes, but not the gloom!
Because from that raw and quiet place
Comes the power to fight and join the race

And run as faaassst! as we did then
Cheetahs springing from our pens
Pumping legs in green fields of joy
We fought the fight. We freed the boy!

Just

I'm just so tired of being told
By those who got it to just not sweat it
'Cause my whole being longs for His fold
And doubts abound I'll ever get it

"Just get out there," they will say,
"Be positive! Just seize the day!"
"I feel for you, really" they next remark
And yet their words just miss their mark

For how can *they* know
That which *we* do not have
How can I prove the negative and show
The *lack of* that has left me halved?

The empty core, for a start
The gaping hole
Where there should *just* be
My beating heart

As shrinks would say, "The basic fault"
As I would say, "The missing key"
That just unlocks for me the vault

That holds the riches of my center
The place where I could – someday – be held
And yet – just now – I cannot enter

So when you speak to me "just"
For me it turns into a "must"
I'm just confused and full of rage
That *I must* now
… alone it seems …
Fill this empty page

Just how describe
Just how confide
Just how explain
This void inside?

And I'm told "It won't get filled."
This abyss into which my being got spilled
"Just don't fret what you didn't get
Mourn it, grieve it, let it go!"
        … and yet…

I stare at the emptiness
The bottomless hole
That swallowed my soul

I'm scared to search down there
Where I'm convinced there is no air
Where I know
Just know
I'll die of my despair

Fall through to nothingness
Confirming, finally, my inner mess

All this grasping for what I never got?
Seems like a smart shot?
Turns out
It's all for naught

Instead
I only get to feel
How really bad it feels
And in that, try to heal

See, I don't get to *get*
What I never got
I get to scream at the vacuum
Of what I'm not

So just how embrace the God
Who visits others in their need?
But on *my* solitary journey
Seems to say "Your soul. *You* feed!"

Just longing for that peace when I wake up
And hoping, humbly, that He can fill my cup

"If you're lost," they say,
"Then just get 'found'
Grace is there. God abounds!"

But my scratched, old record of 40 years
Screams "You're all you've got!"
And my fetid, festering, fucking fears

Get in the way of letting go
And my muddled mind assures me
"He'll not show"

It's just
It's **just**
It's ***just not fair!***
How to build that bridge, midair,
To confidence from dark despair?
When there's just no anchor to bind it there

Just to know who I am
A small hint of His love
A brief glimpse of His plan

Day by day by petty-pacéd day
Frantically trying to find the faith
That He will light my way

Scratching through my mountain of fear
Fighting to feel, to find myself
Before I've lost yet another year

Not just

Not just at all

For "they" just got that sweet immersion
How could they speak the language of desertion?

Fear

"Thank you, Dad, for doing the loans,"
Niko says to me. Inside I groan.
The love and courage he has shown
Convince me that I must atone

Not for my efforts, as it's clear
I *finally* hold him and family near
Trying our ship to safely steer
No, not that.

It's for the fears ...

My founding fear – ABANDONMENT –
It first "left me," alone and spent
And – self-fulfilling prophesy –
Assured, since youth, I'd never see

Those lesser frights that trailed along ...
A nagging line of dreadful ducklings
Quacking for
Their absent Mom

These doubts
They followed
And my insides
They harshly hollowed

And thus inaction –
Hamlet's curse –
Came along
To make things worse

All feeding the maw
Of my self loathing
Justifying the feeling that
"They're all, always going"

Which always led back
Inevitably
Like some hermetically sealed
Greek tragedy

To the callous cruel abandonment
The mother lode, the frozen sun
Whence this leaching loneliness had –
    "Finnegan
    Begin again" –
Begun

As husband/father, I then failed to provide
Money, confidence or pride
And my passion for stories, though it tried
Was long since dropped, set aside

Set aside when family came
But it's myself, not them, I blame
I'd been given no breath to blow the flame
Choked and powerless to shake the shame

So I almost lost everything dear
'Cause I was never *really* here
Those many years of just not *being*
Cowering 'neath the mountain of my fears

And it's for *Niko's* fears
Today that I shed tears
Was this the message
He then, or now!, hears?

To stuff your soul,
Pursue your "goals"
Work hard to earn
Your bread and coal?

Like *my* dad, who one night said to me,
While driving me back to college
That he only kept his soul-grinding job
So that I could gain my knowledge

————————————

I tend to agree
With John Le Carré,
That it's heroic just to live –
Present! – in the everyday

That in this shallow world
That hails "easy" and "recent"
It's extra-ordinary
To be "merely" decent

So for my birthday this year
The best gift of all
Was Niko's simple sentence
That *he* sees *me*
          Standing Tall!

That a 12 year old wrote this?
I can hardly believe
Yet his heart-spoken words
They will spell my reprieve

Written in pen
On a simple card
I try to let in this love
But sometimes it's so hard

For love's opposite
Is fear, not hate
(You can hate the things I do,
Yet still can love me great!)

Fear disconnects
It isolates
It stops our growth
Seals our stunted fates

Like the flower that can't grow
Without ever seeing the sun
So love without connection
Is a song that's never sung

———————————

The dreams, they come to me at night
They tell me to pursue the fight
Rest my head from this prickly plight
Follow my heart to find what's right

And today I *do*, shed the fear, at times
Especially when I write my rhymes
But soon I stop and in a huff
Say "For my sons, this ain't enough!"

For Niko and Alex and my wife
I'll surely settle this sad strife
Gut this "scared shit" with unflinching knife
Let go false fears and *dance* my life

So that by my example
My sons can sample
Connecting love's might
Enabling
      God-like
           Boundless flight!

I wish I'd got
This message sooner
But now's near enough
Hey, I'm a late bloomer!

And I'm passing it on
To my beloved boys
In whose fearless eyes I see
That I too deserve joy!

Roots

My roots shriveled
My wings clipped
So when I read this sage advice
I really kinda flipped

That of all the things we say or do -
We parents who provide for you -
It's "Roots and Wings" our greatest gift
And this thought, for me, caused quite a rift

For looking back, so bleached my soil
Leeched of vitality for this blessed life's toil
Dad scythed from culture, past and family
Mom's brood barren
      (and needing weeding)
            emotionally

So with no fertile feet in rich planted ground
Like a wind-ripped tumbleweed I rolled around
Sustaining sap from proud legacy? Ne'er to be found
Lineage lost, heritage tossed, heir to no crown

Likewise, turning sights skyward seemed
Like trying to mass produce my dreams
To the cold nest, frozen, I would cling
Couldn't close to conceive of spreading wing

No lesson learned about "falling to fly"
Making mistakes? Too scary to try
No ecstasy of upward soaring
      Scraping heaven's sheltering sky
Not even mention of mere ambition
      …And I truly, sadly don't know why

Thus the ironic challenge that I can now spot
Is to give you guys something that I never really got
How best model for your sponge-like souls
Pride in whence I came from, excitement for your future goals?

"Act as if ..." a smiling soothsayer once said
And as I stand on cliff's edge today, filled with dread
So ready to fly free from my rootless, earth-bound head

I passionately pray for you,
My dear beloved boys,
To feel firm the force of forbears fond
Exulting in your imperfect joys

And to have faith that should you fall

You will be caught

and rise instead!

28

Tantrum

I'm getting tired of this poetry shit
It feels a bit like I should quit
'Cause when I read my "suck-up" rhymes
It's clear to me I've wasted time

Pretending to let go my rage
Pretending still to act my age
'Cause what I want to do, you see,
Is throw a fit, cut down a tree

Kick a dog
Pee on the lawn
Break down the door
Of one called Mom

For it was she, *fuck*, can't you see?
Who carefully taught the kid in me
Not to make waves
In her narcissistic sea

So I could never be mad
Could never be bold
Had to solve my own problems
Or be shut out in the cold

When she said "Physician, Heal thyself!"
As a kid I heard "Stay on the shelf"
But in my ears it rang of neglect
        To ask one so young
                Whose life had barely just begun
To be able to truly self-correct

And I realize
As tears well in my eyes
That I so despise
The years of lies

Not to the others
But to myself

The years I couldn't ask for help
The years I couldn't tantrum
The years I couldn't show my pain
Or where I'm really, deeply from

And now?

To let go the fierce hate
That inside made me wait
Made me find my God late
Made me slave to my fate

First I must let myself bleed
Because if the wound
Is bandaged too tightly too soon

The disease's vicious seed
Finds root and eats me inside out
And sends me to my desperate doom

But as I meditate in my quiet room
The healing I pray to be delivered, like a boon,
Will come to me
And set me free …

———————————

I am beating with rage the chest of dad
Who far from mad was rather glad
To have the trust of the son he had

That the anger would not break him
That fear posing as hate couldn't overtake him
And his love for this boy he embraced
Couldn't, wouldn't ever slake in

Any way

The son's tantrum in fact
A way to say

I love you, my Father
And I trust this won't bother
But rather will bind us
One to another

———————————

There I go again, in the poetry,
How I must end on the "up note," you see?
Isn't that a pisser?

But I take it now
As a sign of how
Very much I miss her

So forgive the child
Let him rail
Let him wail
'Cause soon, so soon
        Love will fill his sail

Surrogate

Placeholders, bookmarks, surrogates
Along his journey of starts and fits

"S" the father
"M" the mother
One real sister
And the "group," his brothers

His current tokens
Of verse unspoken
A world with no kin
His "connector" broken

Mother absent in her presence
Dad fades too soon to feel his essence
Sister tangling with teenage turmoil
Brother old, gone. Wound like a coil

The "best friends", unconfided in
Now lost, their lack so chiding him
Classmates who said they wish they'd known
The "him" behind the smile of stone

Then there's the wolf *inside* his door
Howling, hungry, needing more
Like these others a "wet nurse" by name
But suckled in solitary shame

Young, in the pool of life, he tried
To swim, hand clinging to one side
While his "attacher" drowned and died
Yet no one mourned. No one cried

Soon he'll learn to swim the deep
And prays his soul from sharks *He'll* keep
With father, mother, friends he'll weep
Into his heart some warmth does seep

So with these practice parents
And with these fractured friends
He'll grow in his slow way
Means to the hopeful, happy ends

Like with his patient family
The ones who "stuck" and set him free

The wife and sons with whom he's blessed
His chance to leave behind the mess
With them he needn't "pass the test"
Here he can be, can feel ... can rest

And the others?
They'll come with time
As he lives
And hones his rhymes

"But wait!" he says, then stops and thinks
"Again I miss the point. This stinks!
Life ends too soon, like in a 'blink'
These surrogates, *they* are my link!

Enemies

"Thou preparist a table before me
In the presence of mine enemies"
This the foundation of the faith that I seek
God hear me, protect me, deliver me, please

Did You truly make me?
Am I really Your child?
In Your green pastures
May I stay a while?

Restore my soul?
Is that really Your goal?
With waters still
My cup You'll fill?

To feel held in a hostile world
To just know that I'll be all right
To believe in abundance when absence is hurled
Is like asking blind me, "Go. Enjoy the sights!"

Shall I fear no evil in the valley of death?
Shall my soul be anointed with oil?
Shall I ever find the calm in my gut?
Insides that reside in eternal turmoil

Feeling You are *still* there
 - When life is a bear
When all is not fair -
That's what I want, I swear

My enemies are strong, you see
Cunning and baffling and real
And Lord, forgive me, but even you might agree
That your presence, sometimes, is hard to feel

It's the wolf inside me with whom I plead
Yet he pounces despite my cries that he cease
It's the hole inside whose seductive seed
Grows strong and will not my spirit release

Self-loathing and lies – my defects
How can I feed calmly amongst such foes?
Anger, judgment, envy, pride
How let in Your high amongst such lows?

How connect, and not detach?
How accept, and not resent?
How let Your love vanquish my fear?
How not feel shame as I repent?

The straight and righteous path, I know,
Is *not* without danger. To life, that's a taunt!
But the comfort of Your staff and rod
Will reassure me you're there – a caring God

See, 6/23 was my 9/11
My forgotten boy's cry, "Am I part of your heaven?"
So this 23rd Psalm, it resonates
Of the need to feel welcome at Your pearly gates

I pray Your goodness and mercy
Shall follow me
That all my days from fierce wanting
Shall be free

And that to the scared son,
Whispered clear as a bell,
You, wise Shepherd, will say,
"Forever in My house,
        YOU are welcome to dwell!"

Sheep

Schafe können sicher weiden
So sang Sebastion Bach
We sheep are held, Papa J assures me
But sometimes I think that that's a crock

Don't get me wrong, I do so long
For when "Sheep may safely graze"
To me there are so many ways
To feel the beauty in that phrase

Watched over by the Shepherd's gaze
The harmful hand of evil stayed
While His charges freely play
In green pastures dream and lay

But when that kind caregiver leaves
Or worse, is there, but cannot see
The flock, we then prefer to flee
Not *away*, but *internally*

Fighting the fear of his abandonment
Wondering where our trusted keeper went
But, with no direction from those who should,
We often tend to lose our own good

It's the sheep in *wolf's* clothing
Who emerges hence
Protecting himself
At his fellow humans' expense

Instead of praying for help
He preys
Instead of tending his core
He lays

In wait … afraid

And from that dread
Springs fake ferocity
Masking his own feeling
Of paltry paucity

Unable to hold
Alone in the cold
The lost shepherd's load
Of creating safe fold

Becoming, thus, the predator
Stalking salvation
Using things, or worse, others
In his indignation

At the emptiness
The emotional starvation
Turning normal needs
Into toxic conflagration

Destroying with fire
Just to feel heat and light
Fend off the deeper demons
Crouching for him in the inky night

But soon being swallowed
In those false friendly flames
Losing the lamb inside
Forgetting even its name

Donning the mask
Ever fiercer, ever faster
Obeying until oblivion
This ever stricter task master

Until one dreary day
The wolf consumes the sheep
His hide forever hiding
The precious child we've tried to keep

And at that moment
If we're lucky
We curl up
And weep

Mourning the loss
Of who we were
Pleading in scorching sorrow
For our soundless soul to stir

… And maybe, just maybe
Catching wind
Of the scent, heaven-sent?,
Of a strange new friend

Within that wolf who warped us
Wrapped and writhing in his coat
A cub! Newborn, in hope. And torn
About pouncing on unguarded throat

This wolf pup, young, like the lamb,
But not corroded yet by fear
Representing the sentinel's strength
To protect his charges, defend them dear

And if we — we sheep! —
Then nurture this whelp,
Teaching him how each of us
Must first feel held before we ask for help

And, too, absorb *his* lesson
In the positive use of primal power
We find – with grace amazing – look!
The guard returned unto his tower!

Owning the wolf/shepherd
Duo inside us, then
Growing from small, lost boys
Into strong, gentle men

And to know in the fullness of our worldly days,
That in joining light and dark, we will find ways
To feel fine in our skin, no longer crazed,
Shouting, "Yes! We sheep *will* safely graze"

Skin

The snake sheds his skin
As the way to begin
His great belief in
The redemption of sin

Like me who's slithered
Through slime and sludge
Self accuser,
Jury, Judge

Unable often
To shake the grudge
Against myself
    Desperate dark ignominy
    Cruelly barring me
    From that road of happy destiny
    Where I would clearly, dearly
Love to trudge

Wearing unworthiness
Like battle armor
Makes me wonder
If others are more

Able to lose
The constraining cloak
Where I comfortably bleed
Hair shirt raging, red-soaked

Never bothering once
To question the yoke
Of hissing self-hatred
Thorny crown that cruelly pokes

These hellish holes
Upon my brow
But through which, I pray, someday,
Serenity can seep, somehow!

Barbs tearing at the hide
That has kept His peace out
His Forgiving Faith
In *Me*! To Him I now shout! ...

"Slough off this shame
Slough off this fear
Slough off this skin
That binds me here!"

Ever enmeshed
With my fight of the flesh
But in this quixotic quest
Blessed chance to start afresh

Thus like the serpent
So long reviled
I allow myself
A secret smile

For in my heart
Beyond self-damnation
I find clues that I am loved
Even vital in His vast creation

And my wreckage of past?
Can I e'er shed this execration?
To sing with joy "Free at last!"
And believe that declaration

Pair O' Docs

One is smiling and caring
And truly kind
One has clearly, plainly,
Lost his mind

Like Jekyll and Hyde
I must confide
They're both inside
For the wild ride

That famous pair
From the Doctor's lair
Came the one with wild untamed hair
The other with sad and soulful stare

Who were seemingly opposed
Yet really just the same
One twerpy, tethescoped twit
Who went by two kinda silly names

A conflicting conundrum
In humbly human form
Representing our search
For integration when we're torn

(But let's slow it down
Before we go to town
First things first
From least to worst …)

———————————

… Starting in the physical realm
Where I'd like to say
We run across them
Each and every day

In this complex world
Crafted like a fine clock
They're the interlocking gears
The fundamental building blocks

Like light. Right?
It's outta sight!
"It's a wave *and* a particle?"
So read Dad in his article!

A thing *and* pure energy?
Well that for me honestly
Is (not light, but) super heavy
… times eleventy-seventy-three

Or a physics twister so twisted
Even Einstein couldn't fudge it
When immovable object
Meets irresistible force

> As if God created a rock
> So big he couldn't budge it
> Inertia versus energy?
> *Must* I choose my infinite?

Or just smile and surrender
To their singular source

Okay, then try this.
First the egg or the chicken?

I must confess the plot
(And omelete) does thicken
Just as it surely makes
My confused clucking quicken

When I say
"This sentence isn't true"
C'mon now, dude!
Please give me a clue!

Or "If this sentence is true,
Then Santa exists"
Means I'm a'-gittin' my presents!
… even though annoying doubts persist

If you say
"I always lie"
What if it's true?
I wanna cry!

Now I really don't like rules,
But here's one just for you
"Every rule has an exception"
Except this one…true?

"Moderation in all things"
… including moderation?
Means to me that there are times
When excess ain't abomination

Or how about "This page
Is intentionally blank?"
Whoever thought of that
Was playing a sneaky prank

Did you know you can't step
In the same river twice?
Just what does that mean!?
You're really not nice!"

Or "Is it now, now?"
Well, now, that depends…
Question dancing with answer
From now until time ends

———————————

Ever deeper we go
Into the rabbit's hole
Where truth born of perplexity
Is our primary goal

"Man learns from history
That man learns nothing from history"
What a worrisome thought
But can *we* learn from this mystery?

Or if the only constant we humans have
Goes by the name of change
What'd happen then if that constant … changed?
Dunno *de verdad*! It's all too strange.

"The only free people
Know that they're not"
Will keep you spinning bewildered
For the short time you've got

How about
"All we must fear is fear itself?"
So by confronting our terrors,
We can build up fearless health?

Or happiness? – elusive, fickle!
Seek it directly, you're left holding a pickle
Forced intention guarantees evaporation
Rather search out *why* you're here
      And you'll more likely find elation

Dazzling, dizzying
Metaphysical mind twisters
Which fool me and you
(And sometimes even our sisters)

Separate soothsaying surgeons
Who clearly contradict
Yet *both* are and can be right.
Say what? I'm feeling tricked!

Ornery opposites
In the same spot and time
It's against nature's law
It must be a crime!

These differing Docs are quarrelsome
They say "Pick me! I'm the only one!"
But then if I do?
Boy, do I feel dumb!

Puzzled look on your face?
Well confusion is a place
From which we can trace
The greatest gifts
      Of the human race

Like the Zen masters
Who hold the duality
Or those Indian gurus
Attuned to reality

Or others evolved
Much more so than (you? or) me
Who embrace our dear Docs
With harmonious certainty

They know why good and evil
Always arrive together
Comprehend that one without the other
Is like a bird without her feathers

Understand that destiny's a choice
Our uniquely human state
Free will in flux forever
With the fickle finger of freaky fate

They grasp that we must act responsibly
Toward ourselves, our planet, our fellow man
Yet still be able to see with crystal clarity
That it's never just up to our own caring hands

Being courageous and changing
The things that we can
Yet serenely accepting
We don't run the "big plan"

For beyond the purely physical realm
We find this Pair O'Docs at the helm
Of larger barges sailing deeper seas
Of some of life's long-lasting mysteries …

So stick around, won't you?
As we've barely scratched
The surface of
This demented
        Dualistic doctor's
                ID patch …

Abundance

Paradox

… So far we've been much, *much* too tame
Until now playing pleasing parlor games
Haven't spoken the unspoken name
Of these Docs' troubling, bubbling brew of pain

Yes, our Pair O' Docs *is* painful!
There's simply not a doubt
'Cause from the doubt that *they* create
We shout, "Hey I want out!

And we're tempted in such situations
To point at the shadowy infiltrations
Of the one we declare dangerously demonic
Scapegoating horned him whom we find wickedness iconic

Believing that in exorcising
Our devils inside, we're truly prizing
The "good" side we're told will make us whole
Rooting out the "evil" to save our soul

Lynching monsters who've caused us fear
Crushing skeletons who've danced too near
Banishing thoughts we find too queer
Barring emotions that cause us tears

In the deepening dusk we dread such dragons
Whom we feel that we must slay
But from searing sulfery experience
I'm going to suggest another way

A sword to the heart of these "enemies"
We believe brings our problems to their knees
But after conveying this *coup de grace*
We often find that we're most lost

For in piercing this most ferocious Hyde
We often kill off our own life force inside
And left with proper Jekyll then
We discover that we're but half men

So rather than slaughter the secretive one
Accept him and find your true battle begun
The middle ground 'tween light and dark
Is where we build, board by board, our redeeming ark

See, the pain of contradiction
Often makes us change beliefs
And until we calmly hold both truths
We'll never find relief

Like shadows. Though they don't exist
Without us there to cast them –
So our true spirit's often missed
Without our dark side there to blast them …

… blast our fears into the heavens
Throw our doubts into the wind
Open up the crack(pot) in us
To let the light pour in

Each doc *must* drive a part of us,
Yes, it's a runaway bus
So we fidget and fuss
      When we could easily
      Deep breathe-ily
      Simply slowly sigh
      Close our panicked eyes …
And Trust

That in weakness
Will I find my strength
In sitting still
Will I go the greatest length

In surrendering
Will I find my fight
In being vulnerable
Will I build my might

In the eye of the storm
Will I find my peace
In embracing my worries
Will I find release

When I run from life
Will I get the least
Walking toward my pain
Will I help it cease

Making room for others
Lets me find my place
And being there for *them*
Leads me to *my* grace

If we'd only sit still
With these dual docs
Just cope with their conflicts
Without checking the clock

I'd bet a nickel
That we'd find the rock
That they are *both* built on
And so open the lock

That closed the door
When we were three or four
When we could easily walk on
The ceiling *and* floor

They've always been
In you and me
Sharing one trunk
Yet still two separate trees

Two objects in space
Occupying one place
Impossible
Yet, let it be

When we accept the one who's "mad"
Stark and raving. Yes! *Even* bad!
Rather than sad
We find we are glad

In the cosmic chart
They both take their part
Now I can start
  To feel smart!
Letting this soothe
  My aching heart

The crazy one you will agree
Is essential to us, I pray you'll see,
It just don't work, then, when we flee
  So walk toward him
    With open arms
  (He means no harm)
And you'll be free

———

'Cause opposites are often
Not so far apart
In life's laconic circle
We often end up
        Right back at the start

Now sometimes a blessing,
True, is a curse
Sometimes the best
Does mask the worst

But *don't despair*
'Cause you'll discover
More often the curse
Is blessing's mother

Our paradoxical Pair O' Docs delivers
Suffering beautiful and exquisite
And while I realize it's nice to live there, mind,
Sometimes, "Thanks just the same,"
        I'd really rather just visit

And yet my joyful tears
Through all the many years
Would never ever have appeared
Without the gift of grieving dear

It's in our agonizing, anguished moments
That we receive the reward of our truest self
And with that small comfort we can finally rejoice
In finding, through hurting, our greatest wealth

I've found that suffering
Brings out our best
At our apparent lowest
We can rise to the test

When it seems we have no choices
We have one more choice to make
While at the mercy of harsh voices
With our dignity at stake

Piled on by life's misfortunes
That may never seem to slake
With our soul's last drop of decency
We find the courage to face, not fake

When we're distraught we can help others
Despite our pain still shield our brothers
Define our lives, even, by *dying* well
Choosing compassion until the final bell

———————————

Becoming thankful for the rough parts –
In our short stay – that make us who we are
Means tending the fires within ourselves
That are mirrored in the farthest stars

Fathoming these fine physicians
Means accepting each without taking positions
For the wise one he would not exist
Without the weird one's grueling grist

They're the ying and yang
That form me and you
Trace *that* circle
And you'll be less blue

Those great multitudes,
Inside us, thus
Settle down and quiet
Their contradictory fuss

When we grasp
That they're *both* in charge
We find the faith
To live true and large

Accept and let go
And more we'll get
A hard lesson to learn
(And I ain't got it quite yet)

Like knowing my life gets easier
Only when I own that it's hard
Like knowing the strongest pot is formed
From a thousand, tiny, damaged shards

When I understand that my soul must shatter
And that I *will* survive the terrible toll
When I recognize that I'll always be broken
Only then can I become truly whole

It's like when, at times, I escape myself
And finally have the chance to find *me*
Breaking the bondage of my self seeking
That hermetically, brutally binds me

Stepping out of the prison that I call "Steve"
Into the sun that shines so kindly
At last seeing with my heart and not my eyes
That usually do so blind me

———————————

So does one stick with sacred?
Or does one pick profane?
Assume it's one without the other
And you're in for much more pain

Without the dark, there is no light
Without the wrong, there is no right
These daring Docs, once separated
Would mean a world that's grey and faded

One brings the courage of ecstasy
The other of holy sobriety
With both of them in you and me
We grow towards wholeness gradually

Hatred, Wrong, Discord, Error
Rest at our core, yet make us fairer
Doubt, Despair, Sadness, Shadow
Without these we'd never know

That Love, Forgiveness, Harmony
Flow equally into our sea
Those "dark-side" forces of His might
Balance Truth and Faith, Hope, Joy and Light

See, in trying to understand
It appears I'm understood
Find I'm feeling my natural highest
When I focus on someone else's good

Turns out when I comfort
I tend to feel held
Feels like I'm loved the most
When I practice loving well

In self-forgetting
My soul I find
Forgiving others
Myself unbind

But all this goes against my being's every fiber
Making my poor soul shiver and sweat
To trust that He'll hold my dear Docs for me
Throws my battered brain into a dizzying fret

But growing towards my caring God
Means struggling through this paradoxical strife
And in this dying I awaken
      - No. Am reborn! -
            To the significance of precious life

How does this work?
I have no clue
But I believe it's true
For me and you

Align

A line is drawn
In the sand
That asks if I am
"Here" or "there?"

Requiring that
I make a choice
Despite my protest,
"That's not fair!"

Who draws this line?
I do not know
It may be me
Who's trying to throw

Off all the pain
Of being *here*
On *both* sides
Still Stuck in fear

That this border
Self-imposed
Won't shield me
Against life's blows

But nor does it –
Now understood –
Allow me to
Let in the good

So if I can't be
This or that
Why do I still not
Have the sign?

Why is it *still* not
Clear to me
How to *not*
Draw a line?

… Align
That's how
Align myself
Now that's a "Wow!"

Align the "this"
And "that" in me
With visions of
Eternity

Align the "here"
And "there" in me
With His will,
And then I'll see

These lines I draw
Soon washed away
By ocean's of
His love. I pray

That I may have
The strength to be
Aligned with
All His hopes for me

A line: divide? or
Align: bring together?
Living "and" & "yes"
Instead of "if" and "whether"

So rather than feel
I must take sides
"Make the choice
Quick! Decide!"

I pause
And breathe
And raise
My hands

And let
This calm
Smooth out
The sand

No more line!
But now aligned
With His
Kind plan

Waltz!

The Recovery Waltz
        Is the dance
                That I dance
All my days
        All my nights
                From now on.
It's the way
        That I say
                To myself
And my kin,
        "I love you
                From today
                        Til I'm gone."

I just thank
        Him above
                For the love
                        That He shares.
Finally,
        I can feel
                Here and now
                        Be aware
Of how lost
        I once was.
                Now I'm found,
                        Heart laid bare
By these three
        Simple steps
                That I've learned
                        With great care …

"Trust in God"
        "Clean your house"
                "Pass it on"
Simple? Yes!
        Easy? No!
                For in life's
Crazy flow,
        It's so hard
                Just to know
Where my feet
        Next should go.
                So I step
                        Ni-i-ice and slo-o-ow.

"Trust in God"
        Surrender!
                My mind's doubt?
                        Suspend 'er!
'Cause I'm just
        Not in charge.
                Wish I wuz …
                        Tough and LARGE!
I let go,
        Not too late.
                Higher One,
                        My dance mate.
And enjoy,
        Floating free.
                His sure lead,
                        Soothes my needs.

66

Yes, He does
      That for me
           Which I could
Not. You see?
      Baffled less,
           More assured.
Uselessness
      Now is cured.
           And I can
Now be heard.
      No longer
           Alone, but
                  One with His word.

Number two,
      "Clean my house?"
           A downbeat,
                Fruitless feat.
How can I
      Possibly
           Sweep my side
                Of the street?
All my faults …
      Ain't so sweet.
           And for them,
                Make amends
To family
      And friends?
           All those wrongs?
                … Not so neat …

Yet if I
    Stake this pain,
        I've so much
More to gain.
    "Open door,
        To my past."
Seeking self
    Slips away.
        And right now
I can say,
    "Halfway through,
        More serene
            At long last!"

Number Three.
    "Pass it on"
        Now my task?
        My *reprieve*!
Hope? I have
    And strength deep,
        Life lived full.
        So conceive
Fellow beings'
    Fear and pain
        Now my joy
        To relieve
Better give
    Than receive.
        It's so true!
        I believe!

Promises,
    Now fulfilled.
        Waltzing soul,
Now I build.
    And myself
        Discover.
Through His grace,
    His kind cover.
        That it's me,
Not another,
    Who can dance,
        Take the chance,
            And recover!

Fearless

When skyward soars my soul like winged Pegasus,
My heart, let loose its cage, beats tiger bold.
When windows open wide upon the world,
They light a being so lovely to behold

Your touch a jasmine breeze on summer's eve,
Your voice a thousand butterflies in flight,
Your kiss a baby's breath upon the moon,
Your eyes my guiding stars throughout the night

Moment

to catch you in a word
  how discuss your eyes that see all?
to hold you on the page
  how describe your laughter til the tears fall?
to stay you in a sentence
  how portray your love, your heart,
  heaven-sized and once again?
to imprison you in pale poetry
  how imagine your spirit, unbridled,
  seeming always to ascend?

would be diminishment, decrease
of all you are
passion fire movement shoulders swaying
shouting crying slapping caressing
licking sense smell taste sound sight
a sigh

and being
simply being you
being you with me
being a most amazing part of us
alive beyond the bounds of description
a life

Tortuga

She may zzeem zzzlow, but her emotions
Are like powerful life potions
Which when said gives one the notion
That she's deep as any ocean

With all his twitching, the harried hare
Can think himself from here to there
But of one thing he's not aware
That head and heart must always share

For all his hopping and his clawing
All his knowing and his gnawing
Himself in half he ends up sawing
His wish the world that he be awe-ing

Separating soul from spirit
Bind heart to head? Not once comes near it!
'Cause deep down he really fears it
That his own voice? He'll never hear it.

Like that fabled Aesop bunny
Who – sure he was gonna get the money –
Got caught napping in fields sunny
Beat by a tortoise. Now that's funny!

See it ain't how fast we get the goals we seek
How smart we are from week to week
When we stuff far down our feelings, meek
Our truest self we'll never speak

It's the tortoise, steady and slow
Watching the world just go, go, go
Who sooner finds her soul's true flow
Than us rabbits "in the know"

And her shell in which she hides?
Well it holds safe those soft insides
So that for many years and many tides
Her deepest heart she can confide

So from *Mi Tortuga Lenta*
A message from above she senta
Release your feelings from dark tentas
And your joy will not get benta

Cama

Our marital bed
Where not just our minds but instead
Our bodies and our spirits are fed
And to our Creator we are led

For in those moments of diversion
I achieve a rare and real immersion
Feeling part for a moment of the (w)hole ;-)
At one with a sensuous and loving soul

Our sweaty skin a path to His house high
The angels singing in your soft sighs
Blasphemy? Dunno. But I can't deny
That with you I leave the earth and learn to fly

Dawn

You are the Parisian dawn
You are the morning dew upon the lawn
You are eternal love, forevermore
You are the woman I adore

All this and more
We've got in store...

Dancing, earthy, sweaty, real
Loving, hating, present, feel
Mother, wife, lover, strife
In a word, you are LIFE!

Vicky

If I'd been asked a year ago
To speak above a mumble
To show a smile or laugh or sing
Do anything but grumble.

I'd have snapped that, "It's impossible,
It's just not in my nature.
Why should I smile?" I would have grinched
'Til Jeff said "Come and meet her."

One year ago today we met
"I'm Vicki." "Yes, I know."
Since then we've sung our sweet duet
You've set my life aglow.

A snarling Scrooge no more am I
Beating my breast like the thundering sky
For your sun has broken through
And I dance my life anew.

My voice, it has found wing
And bright fanfares now I sing
For we have laughed and we have cried
And we have danced and we have sighed

And as all we've shared whispers in my ear
Like a sweet and soft caress
So the year behind and these many to come
Shout INFINITY! and YES!

Niko

(With apologies to the "Star Spangled Banner")

O say, did you hear
By the dawn's early light?
On July 9th unveiled
Red and healthy and screaming

Now his wails and broad cries
Keep us up through the night
Though his diapers we've washed
After 3 AM feedings

Yet while rocking we stare
At his sleeping face fair
And give thanks for the proof
That a God is still there

O, what will this new-fangled baby yet crave?

If it's praises he wants sung
Then so proudly we'll rave

Happy Birthday
Nikolas Max

Alexcito

When angels dream
    they dream
        the sweet sleep of newborns

When newborns dream
    they dream the dreams
        of downy angel wings

And with their gentle breath
    upon the moon
        fix our stars
            in their knowing smiles
            and melt
                our searching hearts

Welcome Alexander
To our family
And to our world
Made more beautiful by your presence.

Sole

A game for children
Yes it's true
But sort of how I'm
Finding You

While still a baby
Barely hatched
Learning how to
Throw and catch

Feet together
Legs apart
Rolled ball with Dad
Exchanged our hearts

Then stopped playing
With him or Ma
My pre-teen friends
Now made the law

Dorky diamond
Our legs would make
I'd zing the ball
Their nuts to break

Laughing at the
Piercing pain
Connecting yet
Our twisted brains

Now I'm older
Wiser? Maybe …
It's hard to tell …
Than when a baby

Seeking You
As I do now
I'm praying that You can
Smooth my brow

So as I roll my
Ball to You,
My humble thanks
For all You do,

Spinning back
It comes to me,
The joy I felt
At two or three

But there are times,
Yes! My Creator
When heat you throw
And mash my taters

Yet through the ache
I sometimes feel
Your love for me
Is just as real

So up I get
Despite the fear
That somehow you won't
Meet me here

———————————

When Jesus walked
The water then
And crossed the lake
Was it a fake?

Or were You were strolling
Under him?
In perfect sync?!
Yes, there's the link!

Your mirror image
Sole to sole
Makes real
The impossible

How else could I
Who feels the dearth
Be rooted here
To mother earth?

Without Your gravity
At play
I'd long ago
Have flown away

Grounded in
Reality
This solid pressure
Sets me free

From our birth
Until we die
You walk beneath
So we can fly

———————————

Your feet, the feat,
That hold us up
Get us through fear
And fill our cup

So ball to bawl
I start to gain
How much I grow
Because of pain

The "oneness" sometimes
Hard to feel
I still have faith
We're heel to heal

Walk in Your grace
The lifelong goal
To know my place -
We're sole to soul!

Breathe

Breathe, my son
And it will be all right
Rest your head on my heart
And let go the fight

Breathe, just breathe
And forget the fear
That the world is unsafe
Let me wipe your tears

Breathe slowly, surely
Realize that I
Breathe beside you every day
From now until you learn to fly

And breathe, please, when I can't
And it seems that my stress
Is aimed at you
More than the rest

Breathe then most deeply
And your wise soul will sense
That Dad, too, makes wrong turns
In this baffling life, immense

Breathe as well for *my* boy
Who, somewhere along the way,
Was shorn his sturdy lungs
Gasping greatly 'til today

Breathe my faith afresh
Joy just in you, you being born!
Your baby's smile lighting my life
My searching heart no longer torn

Breathe it out
Confusion, doubt
The rage inside
That makes us shout

Breathe it in
The best you've been
Your shining self
Through thick and thin

Breathe in, slow. Breathe out, release.
And as it fills your chest
Know this delicious, dancing air
Is *your* song, singly blessed

Breathe forgiveness
Breathe release
Breathe through sorrows
That never cease

And grasp that in each
Breath you take
My love for you
Will never slake

Focus on this one first need
With wild winds' fury, take no heed
And in that space of grace you'll feed
Your flower bloomed from precious seed

So breathe, cariño, sshhh, now, breathe …
And as I hold you near and dear
Know that nothing else, NOTHING matters!
But you and me. Now and here.

Faith

When the silence falls
Like a deafening blanket
And you talk
A mile a minute
To make sure
You're not alone
I'll be there for you

When the darkness comes
Creeping up the wall
On a Sunday afternoon
And you feel panicked
At losing the gentle light
In the harsh duties of tomorrow
I'll be there for you

Since I flew you, Niko,
Nine months old
Returning from work
Over my head
A raspberrying airplane
You had me
At your electric smile
It's heat defrosting my icy heart
And I am forever there for you

Since you slumbered soundly, Alex,
My clinging baby monkey
Back from a business trip
On my chest
Heart to beating heart
You had me
At your trusting baby's breath
Your soul melting into mine
And I am eternally there for you

I ache
At your absence
Real physical pain
Crumbling my numbed fortress
And it reminds me
That even I, too,
Am alive

Mother bears?
Psssshhhh!
Got nothing
On this Polar Bear Dad
For nothing, my cubs,
Can come between
You and I

So closely
Do I hold you
To my heart

Take these words, then,
With you
And the abiding faith
That leaps from my gut
To yours
Visceral
Tangible

That in your emptiness
I will hold you

That through your deserts
I will be your hidden spring

That when we are together
I am with you

That when we are apart
I am with you

That when you are alone
I am with you

And
      that
            even
                  when
                        I'm
                              gone …

                             I

                  Your father

Will be with you

Always

Dog

(For Bonnie and Teddy …
and all companions greater than ourselves)

Dog loves me unconditionally
She loves me in the now and here
Dog loves me just for being me
She loves me just for being near

This Bonnie love of one foot one
A giant in affection
Smiles on my journey just begun
In Dogliness direction

Dog loves me with joy goofy, free
He loves me with good cheer
Dog's tail loves me so slappily
He loves me without hate or fear

Wild wagging butt, my Teddy bear,
Who leaps when I arrive,
With waving paw says, "There you are!
I'm glad that you're alive!"

Cama[2]

Our family bed
Which in the morn smells just like farts …
    (Sorry, but it's true, I fear
    Today, tomorrow, and all the year)
Is where we go, all four of us
When needing to be held, not feel apart

Tired of the race
The bustle and haste
Snoring face to face
In warmth's embrace

And though the sleep is fitful
With youngest flailing through the night
And oldest stubborn as a pit bull
(In the morning we are quite a sight!)

Baggy eyes
Coughs and sighs

But knowing in our tired smiles
That being together for this while
Makes us stronger one and all
And soothes our souls so each walks tall

Sunday

In that moment
I felt whole
Without the empty ragged freight train
Running through my soul

And it's because of you
That I was there
Floating safely between
Sun and air

Held in your arms
(And His arms too)
Time stopped (for once)
In it's relentless marching through

How to describe
The beauty of being?
The knowing and feeling and
Belonging without seeing?

For we just *were*, you and I,
Naked
Skin to skin
Babes beneath His tender smiling eyes

And bathed in your love
I felt the hole in my center closing up
That gap, that blackness that stares at me
In your arms I barely see

That cave, full of monsters,
That scream out my fears
With your smiling sweet sighs
Barely reach my ears

How express to you in weak words
The feeling of finally being "gotten"
Finally being heard?

In that moment with you
Just where and when and who

I was meant to be

How write with frail language
Just what you mean to me?

Mourning daily these days
The loss of my boy
But Sunday Morning with you
I was lost in our joy

Gorilla
(My Dreams)

A gorilla sits
In the weeds on my street
The strangest sight
I ever did meet

He'd hung from a branch
Near the house above
A hairy souvenir
Of some Tropical Vacation's lingering love

Then he landed below
About a year ago
When our fierce mountain winds
Did howl and blow

They forgot him, I guess
His owners, you see
'Cause they moved away and left him
In obscurity

But there he sat
So regally
Holding silent court
Under the Eucalyptus tree

And to most who passed
While walking their dog
He'd disappear in the brush
Like a bump on a log

But me, *I* would see
His sly secret smile
Daring me to figure out
His cunning Ape-ish wiles

With his palm frond body
And his coconut mouth
  Lazing in the sun
    Shining from the south

      And I'd scratch my head
        And I'd think and I'd puzzle
          "Does he need a home
            Or just a loving monkey nuzzle?"

            Then for a about a month
            He up and disappeared!
            Which, as I ponder on it,
            Was really kind of weird

            Some young teenage kidnapper?
            Or did he take a trip?
            To a gorilla plastic surgeon
            To fix his broken lip?

            And wow! Just now!
            Today, he's come back!
            Like a wise cosmic joke
            Or a winking wise crack

        His arm lounging astride
      The big rock at his side
      As if to say, "Hey!
      I'm here to stay!"

Now that it's apparent
That my happy hirsute friend
Thankfully did not succumb
To a sad untimely end

I take it as a sign
That that Prankster Punk above did send
A kind and gentle message
Of the helping hand *He* tends to lend

So like the willing wind
That one night set Gorilla free
I now seek out these songs
Of soulful serendipity

The happy "coincidence"
That finds me now
I try not to ask of it
Why? or How?

I'd rather peel it
Like friend Darwin's cousin
Sweet bananas like manna
I'll eat by the dozen

It's these mysteries
That allow me to see
They make no sense
But they fill me with glee

They reveal one small part
Of His powerful art
And for some of us
That's a much needed start

On the rocky road back to
Our Grunting

    Grinning

        Primate's

           Primal

              Heart

Prescription

Don't

Run the show
Think you know
Sit in woe
Youth outgrow

Past appeal
Self conceal
Stuff your zeal
Spin your wheels

Do

Work to feel
Self reveal
Humbly kneel
Start to heal

Stretch and grow
Find your flow
Take it slow
Let it go

Belonging

"Your only true possessions
Are your actions," said the wise man
Which when I think about it well,
My brain it kinda fries, man!

'Cause if all these things I "own" right now
Are here but temporary
What offering make my Maker
When I meet Her? Gosh, that's scary!

Defining me
By stuff, I see,
Means "do," don't "be"
And so I plea …

Release this driven, desperate grip
On the false fruits of physicality
Let my humble days be told instead
Not by acquiring, but by morality

Not the deeds we own
But the deeds we do
Pave that golden road
That leads at last to You

It's not the baggage we collect
Nor competing in this life's "tourney"
Rather it's mercy, grace and love
That bring us joy in this brief journey

It's "belonging"
As in what we feel
Not belongings
As in beg, borrow, steal

So give a smile
Like it's a flower
Rain random acts
With kindly showers

Guard children's dreams
From stalwart towers
And never once
Doubt the pure power

Of living simply. *Self*-possessed.
Cosmos beating in our chest
Flying free and fearless 'bove the mess
From *action* whole
       ... and deeply blessed

Abandon

The word screams like a fire alarm
The primal siren, "Hide from harm!"
Or worse than harm, neglect, you see
"You! Tread alone! ... eternally ... "

The sluggish death by thousand cuts
The caring God ... who kneed my nuts
"*Hey*, where did *that* come from?!?" I'd cry
... Yet silence reigned. No answer why.

That bored and dank disinterest
Way worse than hate or all the rest
Of all those feelings I'd let go
Too hard, by far, a row to hoe

So digging down into my hole
My Self I'd bury, like the mole
And seek the me I'd lost ... in others
Dad, son, wife, but mostly mother

Head battering against thick walls
Bowed and bloodied ... I'd fail and fall
And dread, within gates fortified,
I'd find she wasn't on my side

Yet when life's doors *did* open wide
So paralyzed, I'd stand outside!
Frozen by that plaque I feared ...
"Abandon hope, who enter here"

Hope that in my stuckness, still,
She'd finally come, my cup to fill.
So, trapped there, on the threshold stair,
I'd ne'er commit to here *nor* there

Picture it then, this private hell
Where dreams were dashed with no bell's knell
Thrown to the lake, in sealed cage
Pups drowned with silent, in-turned rage

What I'd felt as *my* desertion
Became self-hating, soul immersion
Unknown, unsung, with no lament
Myself I'd left … just up and went

How turn the corner? How find the plan?
That leads me back to human clan
Allow me to give up my dearth
Feet finding, finally, the earth

Well looking deeper I now find
A meaning that escaped my mind
It's funny how small things like this
Can introduce us to our bliss

Abandon also means … *to dance!*
Like no one's watching, take the chance
Expressing joy. Without the fear
That you'll be left by those held dear

Abandon lets me stride in, tall
At ease, erect, and never small
Yet grander, still, than highest peak
Is bending now to help the meek

Abandon means immediate
Saying what I feel, not eating shit
Allowing me to just be me
Not who *you* think that I should be

Abandon is an attitude
Not of fright but gratitude
That letting go, I'll be embraced
Letting God, leads to my grace

Abandon means my Self will out
Emerging bold to laugh and shout
To voice my poems, my childlike rhymes
Roar "Here am I! This is *my* time!"

Abandon helps me "act as if"
I'm not blind and on a cliff
For looking down I'd surely drop
So I just smile ... and start to hop

How climbed I from this purgatory?
More is revealed ... ongoing story ...
The paradox, though, heaven-sent ...
Abandon *now* abandonment!

Tetherball

Boil, boil, toil and tetherball
Bounced back and forth, until we fall
Stirred round and round, this is our all
Stand like the pole? "Boy, you've got gall!"

Whacked dizzily since brewed by Mother
For some of us, our sister/brother
For others it's the kids or wife
Who knock us, zing us through our life

I recollect pouring the concrete with Dad
For the tetherball pole that I once had
In our weedy back yard – so grounded, so glad –
At peace in that moment, at least for a tad

Solidly surrounded by the earth
For that short time I felt no dearth
The tallest I'd stood since tremulous birth
Being, just being me, feeling my worth

And then what happened? The cord got cut!
Steely witch stares that sliced my gut
Since then my ball flew through the air
From fear to numbness to quiet despair

So with nary a tether
I endured wicked weather
With no core to ground me
'Til I banded together

With others who like me
Had lacked that affection
Without early mirrors, hadn't seen our reflection
'Tween our hearts and our heads, had found no connection

Yet side by side, slowly,
Had learned to crawl
To then stand tall
And find our direction

"To feel" is the goal
And through life's cauldren's bubbling toll
Upon my tender searching soul

I emerge

No longer living as the hole
Firmly planted
I *am* the pole

Finally

       Gratefully

              … Almost! ...

                    Whole

How Much I Love You

THE SON

Forgive me,
Mom,
For not
Forgiving you

It's the least -
And quite honestly -
The most
I now can do

THE MOTHER

Forgive me,
Son,
For you
I never really knew

Holding tight
Your precious center
As only
I could really do

If only I had heard
Those simple words
Before you slipped
Into your stroke

Now I've a million
Burning questions
Whose answers

I need spoke

THE HOLY SPIRIT

... you need spoke

But certainly you knew me ...

Not then,
Nor especially now,
So paralyzed and gaunt
It's as if I see right through thee

... knew that I cared ...

No I did not!
And I just find it so unfair!

Unfair?

That you were never there!

Body yes, spirit no
Now past becomes present
Like your addled mind
Damaged, distant, bare

My child
Take care
Of your anger
Be aware

I can't believe - !

And I can't grieve!
Until I face my rage at your neglect
While *your* own growth,
You'd push to perfect!

... I was preoccupied

And so you'd leave your baby there to cry?
Staring from his crib
To a blank and unforgiving ceiling,

Alone, not knowing why?

I was trying to
self improve.

And so you sacrificed *my* youth?

But with you
I'd brag "I got it right"
The "kid thing"
On my third try

Well when I first heard
That from you
One day, out of the blue,
I should have cried

But why?

Mom, don't you understand?
It speaks of me as bus fare
A way to get
From here to there

An experiment
So that you
Could learn
To care!

But self actualization
Is the goal, no?

Not at the expense of those
You've brought onto this earth
… If you then
Just up and go

The more you looked toward self
The more you pushed
<u>Me, who needed you,..</u>   *He, who needed you*

                                   You, who needed me?

… To a far, far back shelf

Trapped in your mirror
With no reflection of my own
A vague, vacillating vampire
Sucking for approval at your throne

                                   Was I not at least
                                   considerate?

Polite to a fault
The fault being
That with your child
Politeness means fleeing

                                   Son. You know how much I
                                   love you.

No I do *not*!
But from you that's the most I got

The words still ringing in my ears
From you who were supposed
       To show,
       Not tell!
       Not riddle,
       But sound love's bell!
And thus allay my sneaking fears …

                                   … That what? I didn't?
                                   Abomination!

Or couldn't
Because it was yourself,
Not me,
The object of your armored adoration

... Explanation? ...

You graduated college at 60 I remember

Friends beaming that you'd B.A'd
After being so long away
Festive laughter and congrats
Loud air kisses and hearty pats

My friends were loyal

Sycophants, maybe, to "Her Royal ..."

But it all snuffed out my ember
My sense of self sliced and dismembered

For both in high school
And in college
When I'd slaved
So hard for knowledge

And adorned my dreary tree
With baubles valedictory
Beta Kappa and Summa cum
Honors up my pimpled bum

Sung leads in plays
Crammed hard for days
Dangled like your marionette
For the love I thought I'd get

A blowout for B.M.O.C.?
Did you celebrate me then?
From you ... ?

                              ... *"Eh. B.F.D."*

A quiet dinner, a fountain pen

So even when earned in The Doing
Greeted coolly ...

                              ... *"Yes, that's fine"*

Much less seen or sung for being
(For concern I might outshine?)

O.K. then, how have I done at life?
The question shreds me like a knife

Self immolated in the flames
Of grasping need for your attention
Achievements drained of meaning
And soul's direction?
            Not even honorable mention

So, so stuck
Without ambition
In meekest muck
Without a mission

Blaming both bad luck
And lack of tradition
"Hey, what the mother f – ?"
My repeated admonition

Thus in confusion and frustration
For aid and comfort I'd turn in

Not seeking help or guidance
As "troubling others" was your worst sin

Since birth, drilled into me, carefully –
And which gold-sealed diplomas
        had officially shown –
"You" ...

... "You, young man,
Should be able, by now,
To figure it out
On your own"

But in trying this tack
My nose got pushed in "the lack"
And so as to avoid a panic attack
Became addicted to a mind drug
        More enslaving than crack

And in these past 5-ish years
Emerging from this thicket of spears
Climbing out from the hole of my empty core
And still kicking my demons out the door

I know I've grown
And God has shown
Me His kind light
So I can fight

This battle now
To let go, somehow
And say, "Yes, it was rough,
But I am enough!"

But this?
How now?
I thought I taught you
"Be not proud!"

110

And that message stuck
Clear and loud
And long I've worn it
Like a shroud

For withholding from your oven's bun
Is callous, cruel. Creating in him
The constant sense of life forever
Unbegun

I can't believe ...
I'm stunned!

Just listen to your son

I see a vision of your skirt, it's pattern near
Plaid scratchy wool that itched my ear
But why does it now surface here?
       Oh yes,
Because your lap so rarely would appear!

Overpoweringly would I yearn
To lay my head there, somehow return
To womb's warm haven pleading –
       "Have *this* I not yet earned?!" -
The constant dread of being spurned

But, why have you turned - ?

Because doubts yet persist
That I – *Listen up!* – am even meant to *exist*
And now it's getting me kinda pissed
That still for me it goes on like this

So what?
You'd give me your fist?

Mom, it's no longer about you, I'm sure
And this is my point: nor is it any longer even
About the who that you were

It's now about how best to cure
The you I hold in me. How dig out
From 'neath my skin
These voracious, vicious, vexing burs

All meaningless
Matronly slurs.

The critic pushes away
So she won't get hurt
Protecting herself
With words cutting and curt

Forever finding fault
With flaw-seeking eyes –

Self defense!

Self defense?

It was simply self-defense!
Don't you – Can't you realize?

Bringing others down
In your need to get ahead?

Leveling the playing field
So my shriveled soul could get fed

But the damage downstream?
To your own spawn who bled?

Purple is my favorite color
Ice blue and blood red

112

I don't believe you so callous. No.
Perhaps just fleeing your founding fear?

Fear truly drives us both, my dear

You *and* me?

Breath by breath
Year after year

The common ground comes clear
Let hope appear
Let love come near ...

Let healing happen here
Let healing happen here
Let healing happen here
Let healing happen here

For if ...

... <u>My mother</u>   ... *<u>My mother</u>* ...

... Could never really ...

                                        ... *see "the other"* ...

... Because the neediness ...

                                        ... *inside her* ...

... Was all she had ...

                                        ... *to guide her* ...

... Bereft of tender ...

                                        ... *sanctuary* ...

... Like hurting Jesus ...

                                        ... *in the arms of Mary*

Then you not only fear ...

                                        .... *that you don't belong
                                        "here"* ...

... But too <u>with God</u> ...   ... with me ...

                                        ... *and parent plea* ...

"<u>Was I ever really
meant to be</u>?!?"   *"<u>Was I ever really
                                        meant to be</u>?!?"*

114

And so you hoard …

… those scraps left on the cutting board

…and though unseemly,
"untoward" …

… master soon the swift, pre-emptive sword

Rapier sarcasm …

… or exasperated sighs …

… Unimpressed …

… or unforgiving eyes …

And thus my child who tries …

… and tries …

… and tries …

… is left alone …

… banging head …

…on walls of stone …

Aching always …

… to atone …

For what sin?
I've never known …

For what sin?
I've never known …

Adrift ...

...he cries ...   ...they cry ...   ... *she cries*...

And so as not to die...

...builds strong his shield   ... *builds strong her shield*

... self defending ...

...forever wandering ...   ... *forever wandering* ...

... quest unending ...

... forever wondering ...   ... *forever wondering* ...

... not apprehending ...

...why?   ...why?   ...*why?*

So, unlike your guarded phrasing,
This, how much *I* love *YOU*. Praising
With simple gratitudes for you
That show *my* feelings through and through:

Thank you for the writing, Mom
It's now my way of fighting on.
Thank you for the words I wield
They've helped to melt my prickly shield

Thank you for my searching brain
Still seeking truth through all this pain
And knowing (though oft self-despised)
With help   With help
I'll overcome the lies   We overcome the lies

116

Thank you for my self reliance
Though sometimes seen as daft defiance
It's taken me far in the physical realm
(Though now it's time   To me you now
To relinquish the helm)   May relinquish the helm

Thank you for creative vision
Connections made. Inventive fission
That rescued me with thinnest thread
Saved my soul   Saved your soul
From all that's dead   From all that's dead

Thanks, then, for what you were able to give
These lessons learned have helped me live

"If you want to keep it,"
They say, "Give it away!"   Give it away!
Thus I'll pass these on
Each and every day   Each blessed day

So now and here
I, in this hour,
Release you to   Release her to
His healing power   My healing power

And pray that in
My letting go
His love for you   I'll love you both   His love for me
You'll surely know   You'll surely know   I'll surely know

From round your throat
I'll loose my grip
Into His arms   Into my arms
You'll gently slip   I'll gently slip

117

Because within
That loving act   That loving act
I can't deny
This simple fact

That you'll then feel   You'll both feel
With all your heart   With all your heart
Serenity   Serenity
Whole. Not apart.   Whole. Not apart.

Allowing *Him*   Allowing me
To heal the wound   To heal the wound
To which *I've* been
So deeply tuned

Releasing you
Releases me
From bonds of self   From bonds of self
Finally set free   Finally set free

Forgiving you   Forgiving ...
Unchains me from   Unchains you ...
This lonely life
From which I've come

Allows at last   Allow at last
His love to rain   My love to reign
Upon my fields   Upon my fields
So parched with pain   So parched with pain

And now regain
The me in me
The fullness of   The fullness of
My being set free   Your being set free

118

We'll finally feel	You'll finally feel	*We'll finally feel*
How much He loves us	How much I love you	*How much He loves us*
He's at our side	I'm at your side	*He's at our side*
Not high above us	Not high above you	*Not high above us*

With my embrace ...

With his ...

                                                ... embrace ...

... we'll rest ...

                                                ... in place.

Look!

                                                ...see His face?!

My precious God!

Welcome home!

Thank you, God!

| Redeeming grace | Redeeming grace | *Redeeming grace* |

FOR MORE

For audio recordings of select poems and
more information on the author
and upcoming works, please visit:

www.PoetStevieG.com

or for feedback email

StevieG@PoetStevieG.com

… and one final appreciation for Mr. Geisel

Yes, the (better or) verse flew loud and loose
When I finally found my inner Seuss
So at the real risk of hero abuse
I simply say, "Thanks, Dr. Silly Goose."

ABOUT

A Southern California native, what Stevie G does to feed his family has ranged from two decades of producing documentaries and commercials to another decade in home sales and finance (understandable for a guy who's always been trying to find his way "home"). What he does to feed his soul is write poetry and children's books (with the requisite screenplay or two in the attic). Having slowly begun to feel less a stranger in a strange land - i.e. planet earth - his other joys come from walking the spiritual path with the wise and radiant love of his life, Victoria, raising together their two beautiful boys, Nikolas and Alexander, and in learning … oh so gradually … to live one day at a time through the example of the family's ferocious midget mutts, Bonnie and Teddy.

www.ingramcontent.com/pod-product-compliance
Lightning Source LLC
Chambersburg PA
CBHW031515040426
42445CB00009B/240

* 9 7 8 0 6 1 5 9 3 5 9 3 5 *